For

Sister Teresa Margaret
    of the Sacred Heart, D.C.
    our song for your singing
    on this your glad day of
    final profession.
        Yours in the Holy Cross
            Sister M. Madeleva

The Feast of Saint Michael
    1942

SELECTED POEMS

THE MACMILLAN COMPANY
NEW YORK · BOSTON · CHICAGO · DALLAS
ATLANTA · SAN FRANCISCO

MACMILLAN AND CO., LIMITED
LONDON · BOMBAY · CALCUTTA · MADRAS
MELBOURNE

THE MACMILLAN COMPANY
OF CANADA, LIMITED
TORONTO

SELECTED POEMS

BY

SISTER M. MADELEVA

NEW YORK
THE MACMILLAN COMPANY
1939

P
M

Set up and printed. Published March, 1939.

Reprinted November, 1939.

PRINTED IN THE UNITED STATES OF AMERICA
AMERICAN BOOK—STRATFORD PRESS, INC., NEW YORK

TO
Manhattan College
in allegiance

ACKNOWLEDGMENTS

*A number of the poems in this
volume are reprinted through
the courtesy of the*
Appleton-Century Company,
America, Ave Maria,
Catholic World, Commonweal,
Franciscan, Spirit.

CONTENTS

Summaries

xi

CHRONICLE

LIMITATIONS

Words I can pattern
Row after row.
How to plan a snowflake
I do not know.

I can fashion raiment
For me, for you.
But to clothe a pansy
What can I do?

I can plant a garden,
Set its paths with care.
Who will tell a dawn wind
To wander there?

I can fly forever
Where my love may be
And no bird, no thought can
Follow me!

LOVE AND THE LAW

Your word is law. You lift these high horizons
Of mountains; stretch this long line of the sea;
Set me enamored and elate between them;
Then, with a breath, you take them all from me.

Your word is still my law. I vow to follow
What path you point, whatever trail you show.
Take when you will these blue stars of December,
This strange and silent loveliness of snow.

No, I retract. I will not sell the ocean;
My mountains and the blossoming stars above;
Peace and the snow and all my wild, white freedom
Except you swear by God your word is love.

RIDDLES ONE, TWO, AND THREE

My lover is a fool more wise
Than Solomon;
My lover is a bird that flies
Into the sun.

He is a lighted lamp, my love,
A midnight cry,
A mortal worm that died to prove
He could not die.

My lover is a cedar tree
With branches spread;
A sweet and bitter fruit is he,
Alive and dead.

My lover is a quiet rain
Falling on fleece;
My lover is or endless pain
Or endless peace,

Or sometime an instinctive mole
Breaking the clod;
My lover is a thief who stole
The name of God.

PENELOPE

Penelope never has raveled as I have raveled;
She never has fashioned the fabrics that I have spun;
And neither her heart nor her lover has traveled as mine
    has traveled
Under the sun.

Her web of delay, deliberate, passionate, splendid,
Was tense with allurement, I doubt not; was wet with
    tears;
But love found it raveled, unfinished—a burial robe—
    and ended
Those piteous years.

My fingers run wildly through warps of bewildering
    wonder,
Or dream over woof of caught silence or sudden song;
They tighten on patterns of laughter or fear that is
    stricken thunder!—
O Love, how long?

Is it naught that I pause in my web as yon suitor woos
 me;
That I ravel at night with regret the design of day;
That loneliness sickens, grief dazes, and doubt pursues me
With you away?

With a lifetime of years do I lash myself to you and bind
 you,
Do I dare all the seas of the world without compass or
 star;
Past the lands of Calypso and Circe and Scylla I seek you
 and find you,
Be it never so far!

So I fare on the deific pathway my love has traveled
As I fashion the web that Penelope could not have spun,
And ravel the heavenly robe of delay that she could not
 have raveled
Under the sun.

A QUESTION OF LOVERS

There be lovers who bring me roses, the velvet of buds
    upcurled;
But only one lover gives me the blossoms of all the world.

There be those who have pearls, have rubies; but much as
    I care for these,
This night will my true love bring me the moon and the
    Pleiades.

I have tokens, if gifts could buy me, till love and its quest
    be done.
Who will catch me a cloud's white splendor; who will
    fetch me the dying sun?

Or who, on the wings of the morning, will hasten, when
    dawn is sweet,
To meet and possess me solely? One only, with pierced
    feet.

And who, for he loves me truly, will give me as token this,
This poignance of love unspoken, two wounds in his hands
    to kiss?

YOU ASK MY AGE

I am older than dawn
And sunset are.
I can think past the light
Of the oldest star.

The piled-up mountains
And ancient trees,
Timeless rivers
And ageless seas;

East and west winds,
South and north:
I know the hour
That brought them forth.

How old am I?
As days are told,
The earth is younger
Than I am old.

Years cannot measure
Time for me.
Fetch us the clock
Of infinity.

This is the answer
If you would know;
From life I come;
To life I go.

Wherefore I am
More gladly young
Than a child not born,
Than a song not sung;

More young than the spring
Before its birth,
Than the dreaming life
In the dreaming earth;

More young than the hosts
Of seraphim
Who sing, "Hosanna,
Elohim."

Older I am
Than any star
And younger than
The angels are.

TRAVEL SONG

Know you the journey that I take?
Know you the voyage that I make?
The joy of it one's heart could break.

No jot of time have I to spare,
Nor will to loiter anywhere,
So eager am I to be there.

For that the way is hard and long,
For that gray fears upon it throng,
I set my journey to a song,

And it grows wondrous happy so.
Singing I hurry on for oh!
It is to God, to God, I go.

A LETTER TO MY MOST HIGH LORD

This letter do I write to Thee,
My Lord most high,
To say I love Thee and to make
A quest hereby.

Thou knowest that Thy mother is
My Lady dear;
Thou knowest that I make small songs
For her to hear.

Of late my little singing words
Have fled away,
And she has had no song, sweet Lord,
This many a day.

Wherefore I ask Thee, do Thou bid
Some angel bring
Unto my Lady dear the songs
I cannot sing.

Oh, let it be an angel small
With simple ways
Who will not feel it mean to chant
My childish praise.

This is the quest, my Lover Lord,
With which I come;
And though Thou strike my tongue, my heart
Forever dumb,

I will exchange for sweets of song
One thing more sweet,
The silence of adoring lips
Against Thy feet.

A YOUNG GIRL WRITETH TO HER FATHER

My Father, I wrote Thee sometime a letter.
Dost remember,—the matter was on a song?
But now I would ask Thee for something better,
A thing I have waited for long and long.

I know full well that upon my pleasure
The veriest thought of Thy heart is bent;
I know that Thou givest me without measure
All that can bring to my soul content.

This country, sweet Sire, whither Thou hast sent me
Is passing lovely and fair to see;
It should, in truth, if aught could, content me
Away from home and apart from Thee.

But ever a golden shadow falleth
Whither-so-ever my child heart turns,
And a voice as of many waters calleth,
Calleth—O Sire, how my wild heart burns,

Knowing not why; and then I am lonely,
Lonely where erst I had happy been,
Homesick for Thee and desiring only
To see the face I have never seen.

Now I close with love, hoping Thou wilt borrow
Some little moments to answer me,
Sending me word that upon the morrow
I may come home, Father, home to Thee.

THE THEME

Always the selfsame word, day upon day;
The little songs I sing, the prayers I pray,
My boldest thoughts of Thee run all one way:

"I love Thee,"—ever, ever, "I love Thee,"
Until I fear that Thou must wearied be
To have no other speech than this from me.

What sayest Thou, sweet my Lover?—"Do not I
Tire of the tireless sun, the constant sky,
The faithful stars forever slipping by?

"Doth it not vex Me that upon the beach
The tides monotonous run? Will I not teach
The never-changing sea some newer speech?

"Am I not weary that all trees are stirred
By willful, changing winds; that every bird
Hath but a single, albeit a liquid word?

"Nay, should I tire of seasons and the sun,
Till time its last, unfaltering course hath run
Tell Me thou lovest Me, My precious one!

"When, on some ultimate day, in sudden bliss
I catch thee to My heart in death's fierce kiss,
I shall have naught to say to thee but this:

" 'I love thee, love thee!' Wilt thou wearied be
To hear thy poor, one word eternally?"
Nay, changeless One, it is enough for me!

Enough, too, this, that Thou shouldst bid me say,
"I love Thee," till the shadows flee away,
Till light dissolves the darkness and the day

Breaks, and upon the waiting silence thrills
Thy word forever, and its glory stills
The yearnings of the everlasting hills.

OF DUST

I said to my body, "Be mindful thou art an offender,
Thou art dust of the dust, thou art slime, thou art clod
    of the clod."
But my body made answer, "O soul, I am blind with the
    splendor
Of the promise of God."

"Methinks, O my body, that thou shouldst be compassed
    with sadness,"
I said, "who hast tasted of life and must yet taste of
    death."
"But know, I have breathed," said my body, "to ecstatic
    gladness,
The breath of God's breath.

"And this clay will pass from me, and life, aye, and
    death, like a vapor;
I shall rise at His word, light as light, quick as thought,
    swift as wing;
For though dust, soul of mine, even dust in the hands of
    its shaper
Is a glorified thing."

—AND SO I AM BETRAYED

You spoke of loneliness before I went;
You knew that I would be too proud to show it,
In which security I was content.
You did not say the mocking-bird would know it.

Longing you mentioned in a casual way;
You thought the sea and mountain-trails might bring it;
Knowing, you were too merciful to say
The mocking-bird, the mocking-bird would sing it.

Hunger and thirst and loneliness have come;
This wild, this poignant singing has unmade me;
It is not pride but longing holds me dumb.
The mocking-bird, beloved, has betrayed me.

THE LIGHT

You do not know; you cannot, cannot guess
Across what burning sands I came to you;
Over what difficult hills, upon what new
Hard ways of loneliness.

You did not think of gifts—my piteous three;
Worthy I thought them—kings had such of old—
Do you keep but the frankincense and gold,
And leave the myrrh to me.

Bid me, I will return into the night;
Remember only, you who merciful are,
I found you by the shining of a star,
So must I walk forever in its light.

FOR YOUR BIRTHDAY

Dear, I would spread the wide earth for your table
And light the stars for tapers, every one;
And kindle, at their dying, were I able,
The lordly sun.

And I would set a banquet for your pleasure,
Brave with brave things my soul is dreaming of,
Glad as my heart is glad, above all measure
Sweet with my love.

But through the dawn I see two candles burning
At a white board where you with Christ are fed;
Lo, how your heart is filled and all its yearning
Is comforted!

WHITE PEACE

The whiteness of the moon is on the world,
Sleeping and beautiful;
Across the blue remoteness drifts and clings
The wandering whiteness of a single cloud.
One passionless mountain lifts its face to heaven,
Wrapped in white peace and very far away.
To the quick bosom of the earth is pressed
The fragrant whiteness of a little flower.

The light of your white soul shines on my life,
And in my heart the whiteness of your love
Burns always.

FUTILITY

I have to dress you in your shroud
    (A crude device, by no means new)
And look on you who are so proud
To worms consigned, to ashes bowed,
To keep my heart from loving you.

I have to call your faults by roll
    (Who once had sought to find them few)
To scrutinize your flaws of soul,
Then memorize and cite the whole
To keep myself from wanting you.

And when I painfully have taught
My mind to scorn you and forget,
I look upon the thing I've wrought
So futilely. It comes to naught.
I love you and I want you yet.

TO THE INITIATE

My kiss upon your brow,
Subtle and cool and continent,
Is two parts vow
And two parts sacrament.

But to your lips I press
Only the white flame of desire;
If two parts are caress,
Two parts are cleansing fire.

Because you understand
This word beyond life's weak replies,
Beloved, take my hand;
Beloved, close your eyes.

COMMUNION

Having held you
I have held whiteness intense and austere as the snows
    that rest
On that far, lone mountain, against my breast.
I have held whiteness more shining and splendid than
    clouds that start
In still skies of summer, upon my heart.
I have held whiteness more wistful and dear than a child's
    alarms,
Than a flower upfolded, within my arms.
I have held whiteness that burns like a flame, that broods
    like a dove
In my soul forever, I have held love.

THE SWIMMER

Afraid? Of you, strong proxy lover, you, God's sea?
I give you my small self ecstatically,
To be caught, held, or buffeted; to rest
Heart to your heart, and breast to breathing breast;
To know on arms and cheeks, on brow and lips the bliss,
The stinging madness of one infinite kiss;
Daring your most exquisite, sweet alarms
In the safe compass of the everlasting arms.

IN DESERT PLACES

God has a way of making flowers grow.
He is both daring and direct about it.
If you know half the flowers that I know,
You do not doubt it.

He chooses some gray rock, austere and high,
For garden-plot; trafficks with sun and weather;
Then lifts an Indian paintbrush to the sky,
Half flame, half feather.

In desert places it is quite the same;
He delves at petal-plans, divinely, surely,
Until a bud too shy to have a name
Blossoms demurely.

He dares to sow the waste, to plow the rock.
Though Eden knew His beauty and His power,
He could not plant in it a yucca stalk,
A cactus flower.

THE PEPPER TREE

On a night the sun and the earth and the weather
And their brother, the wind, all slept together.

And it happened while they were slumbering
That each one dreamed of a different thing,

And then awoke.
The wind first spoke.

"I dreamed," said he,
"Of a fairy tree."

"And I," said the weather,
"Of a fairy's feather."

Spoke the earth, "My dream
Was all agleam

"With rubies red
Of fairies." Said

The sun, "Mine made
A fairy glade
Of delicately woven shade."

Then they laughed, did the sun and the earth and the
    weather
And the wind, as they put their dreams together.

But I wonder if ever these gay lads knew
That the pepper tree on that same night grew.

YOUNG MOON

He comes, a gay and golden star
Climbing the topmost hills of night;
Past where white mountain summits are
He takes his perilous path of light,
Gallant and bright.

A cavalier of plume and curl
Is he, upon his lady's quest;
Look where she goes, exquisite girl,
In whiteness of shy silver dressed,
Walking the west.

THE FOOLISH SENTRY

Night and the stars have come to town.
The wind walks up; the wind walks down,
Beneath my window, beside my door.
The wind knows not what the night is for.

He frights off sleep, the comforter;
He fights off sleep, the ravisher;
He lets no ghost of a dream pass by.
What though I wait for sleep, the spy,

To bring me a word of oblivion,
The wind will watch till his watch be done!
Never shall I consort with sleep
While he has the ward of my gate to keep.

Sentry, why do you stalk my door?
Waking is not what the night is for.
Fool, let my gate unguarded be
That sleep, the blessed, may come to me.

MEDITATION ON ATLAS

Atlas held the firmament
But could not see the sun;
He had the world between his hands
But did not have its fun.

He ate the bread of bitterness
Nor knew that bread is sweet;
Nor guessed the joy of outstretched arms,
The gayety of feet.

The earth was on his shoulders;
The sky was on the earth;
He did not know its wonder;
He did not know its mirth.

He knelt for aeons, burdened
With the whole unwieldy scheme
And he missed the point entirely
Of the grand, deific theme.

I have hung for years together
On a stark, two-branching tree.
It holds the earth and sky apart;
It binds them endlessly.

My tree becomes a table;
I have tasted of its food;
I have eaten of God's body;
I have dared to drink God's blood.

I am stretched out and uplifted
Among stars and planets piled
In the anguish of the prophets
And the weakness of a child.

I can hold the earth for Atlas
And the skies above his head;
I can hold the God Who made them
And He will not strike me dead.

Be strong and glad as God is;
Open your great arms wide
And set your feet against God's feet,
Atlas. Be crucified.

FROM AN AFTERNOON CALLER

I called at your
New house today
To hear the words
You do not say;

To watch the eyes
I cannot see,
The hands you do not
Give to me.

I waited there
A quiet while
In the lost wonder
Of your smile,

And found a home
Austere and new
That has enshrined
And hallowed you.

I love this house
Where you are dead.
Your new grave leaves me
Comforted.

35

I WILL REMEMBER RAHAB

Rahab was a harlot and lived in Jericho;
Neither was respectable. That was years ago.

She had no scented virtues; she told easy lies;
Her practice was flagrant. Once two spies

Came to her door, their lives at stake;
She took and hid them for the Lord God's sake.

They left her house; they left the town;
The next thing she knew the walls fell down.

She hung a scarlet cord from her window ledge;
It was her sign; it was their pledge.

She heard the trumpets; she heard the shout
Of people in tumult, of city in rout.

The men and the women, the young and the old
Were killed by the sword, so I am told;

But her father and her mother knew no ill
Because of the cord at Rahab's window sill.

I remember Rahab to this day,
And I honor her womanhood for all you say.

It called for mercy and it called for pluck.
You wouldn't think a harlot would have such luck.

FROM THE BOOK OF ESTHER

"Give a fool rope"—the saying goes;
Aman has enough, I suppose.

On his own gibbet, twenty ells high,
He dangles now between earth and sky.

Mardochai rides, by the king's decree,
In silk sky color for the world to see;

And my people, suddenly snatched from death,
Dream not the hazard that bought them breath.

Meanwhile, I in a royal garden
Change my life for their peace and pardon;

Change by the accident of beauty
A girl's young self for a brave queen's duty.

Beauty was all I had to use,
And life was little enough to lose,
And happiness nothing at all to choose.

Jehovah lighted my beauty's flame.
It shall burn for the king in Jehovah's name,
Returning to beauty whence it came.

What matter who reads in this thing that's writ:
"Beauty and youth and a little wit
And a rope with a fool at the end of it!"

OF WOUNDS

I have no word to match with its white wonder,
The garment of His body as He wore it
On that first dawning that He came to me
After His death.

Some things there were the soldiers played at dice for,
Kirtle and cloak, perhaps; each got a part
Of such dear raiment as He had about Him,
But not this single garment that He wore.
For that was mine, out of my body woven
Into the pattern of the Son of God,
Seamless from head to foot, and perfect;
Growing to fit His growth, strong with His strength,
Until the day He died.

That day the soldiers tore it, soiled it, spat upon it,
Flayed it to shreds, seared it with gaping rents.
Being His mother, I shall not forget it.

Only for joy I did forget on that first morning
That He returned to me, clad in its splendor
Cut from the loom of death.

Being His mother, I had wished His body flawless,
Fearing to think how beautiful might be
Five open wounds upon it.
I know now that they are as beautiful as God.

Seven expert and competent devils have harassed me all
the day!
They have knotted so deftly my hair I can scarce unbind
it;
They have hidden my most subtle perfume; I cannot
find it.
My lips they have reft of their kisses, my eyes of their
tears;
My heart they have stricken with hardness; my soul they
have shaken with fears;
And the end is not yet, possessing what power they do
over past, over possible years.

In the presence of anguished chagrin, in the face of
familiar dismay
I have little to say.
I have doggedly faced the sharp issue, exploited, defined it.
Their nice malice I guess and defy once for all! What if
now I should humanly mind it?
They are devils at best who beset, but who never, who
never
Can touch my sure peace. I despise them and daunt them
forever!

Let them measure efficiency's utmost by every device they
    may know or possess or discover.
I have one foolish weapon of love. I have Christ for a
    lover.

IN THE WAY

Held eyes and foolish hearts had they
Who walked to Emmaus the day
The dead and deathless Son of God
Beside them as a stranger trod.

Perhaps it was a way with them,
For often in Jerusalem
Their ears had listened to a Word
Nor understood the things they heard.

Their eyes had seen in Galilee
Wonders that prophets longed to see;
Their hearts had stirred to fear and doubt
Things that must make the stones cry out.

Such wonders and such wonderings
Were no uncommon happenings.
Slow hearts, unseeing eyes they had
The while they pondered and were sad.

But know you, this had come to pass:
Their hearts had smitten been as grass,
And their poor eyes beggared of sight
For looking on unveiled Light;

And they had died of seeing God,
Had He not been in lowness shod.
I think He walks beside me thus
What times I go to Emmaus.

I ENTER OXFORD

It was a bird first spoke to me at Oxford
Through the white fog a single, tentative word.
There were, that daybreak, in my new world only
I and a bird.

I had no grateful syllable to answer,
No littlest sign to say I understood
That lyric word to me, more brave than sunlight,
More kind than food.

Oh! there are bells and there are spires at Oxford,
Ancient, heartbreaking, wordless, splendorous things;
Only to me belongs this simple, silver
Welcome on wings.

CHERWELL RIVER, OXFORD

I am a silken highway none walks upon
Only, in beauty going, you, white swan,
Through the clear dawn.

I am a sleeping mirror, unconscious till
You lean above my face to gaze your grave eyes' fill
In me, silver-still.

I am a dreaming fountain, limpid, cold,
Sealed, save to you. Come, beauteous, bold,
To me to hold.

SURVIVORS ON THE FRENCH RIVIERA

The aloe can have died of blossoming
A hundred times and more
Since dream-and-travel-dazed Odysseus
Wandered this shore.

The punctual cypress can have sought the sun
Through seed and faultless spire
A hundred times since one has watched beside
A Roman fire.

A thousand years ago these low Alps knew
The dark moods of the Moor.
Of crescent, empire, or of Ithaca
Who can be sure?

There have survived these low Alps and the sky,
Mistral and ocean swell,
I and this delicately blossoming field
Of asphodel.

THINGS TO BE LOVED

The Carceri, soft rain in February,
These two stone oaks, this sky of Giotto's blue,
Beds of hepatica and fritillary
In this square garden plot that Francis knew:

These things are to be loved. I know. I love them
In their still world, uplifted from the plain.
I choose for you the diffident dearest of them,
White fritillaries in the Umbrian rain.

SUEZ CANAL AT SUNSET

Two long, low, level banks of sand and a long, low sky;
On a strong, straight leash of water a thoroughbred boat
    goes by.
Far to the south a single cluster of palm trees lifts itself
    like a cry.
Across the long, low, shifting levels and hills of sand
    comes no reply.
The light in the west that was gold and rose is dead now.
    I watched it die.

I VISIT CARMEL

Your eyes of infinite kindness meeting mine,
Your hand of quiet resting in my hand
Had been as comforting as oil and wine,
As sweet as water in a desert land.

But in this still room, hopelessly serene,
Why should I seek you, difficult and dear;
In these strange silences with peace between,
How should I vainly think to find you here?

A voice as luminous and cool as dew
Is near me, though I saw not whence it came;
And you are here, sweet, inexplicable you,
Making miraculous music of my name.

Your voice, precursor in my wilderness,
More blessed is, more clear than sight to me;
If there be beauty else I cannot guess,
When you have healed me and when I shall see.

Only I know beatitude begun;
Only I feel no let of cloister bars;
For I have seen a splendor past the sun,
Have heard a voice beyond the listening stars.

THE SHOPPER

I knew the hills of Nazareth
Had miracles to tell.
I hoped the shops of Nazareth
Had memories to sell.
I climbed the streets of Nazareth
And bought a camel's bell.

At Cana's well in Galilee
One draws no wine today
And wedding guests in Galilee
Have no great word to say.
A beggar child in Galilee
Sold me a pot of clay.

In cobble-stoned Jerusalem
For hours and hours I stood.
I brought back from Jerusalem
The simplest thing I could,
A donkey from Jerusalem
Cut out of olive wood.

A house of bread is Bethlehem
And though I came from far
I did not shop in Bethlehem
Except to buy a bar
Of sunset over Bethlehem
And the first evening star.

GATES

The oranges at Jaffa gate
Are heaped in hills; men sell and buy
Or sit and watch the twisted road
Or David's tower against the sky.

The Golden Gate is walled with stone.
No king can pass nor prophet see
The valley of Jehosophat,
The olives of Gethsemane.

St. Stephen's is a quiet gate,
A simple door that lets in dawn.
Its hill, its walls, its ancient stones,
What strange things they have looked upon!

Asses, belabored, stumble past;
Traffickers clamor; priests debate;
A child begs alms; a blind man gropes
To sunshine at Damascus gate.

The world has narrow gates and wide;
Men seek their loves through all of them
And I have come here, seeking mine,
Jerusalem, Jerusalem!

SONG SILENCE

Yes, I shall take this quiet house and keep it
With kindled hearth and candle-lighted board,
In singing silence garnish it and sweep it
      For Christ, my Lord.

My heart is filled with little songs to sing Him.
I dream them into words with careful art.
But this I think a better gift to bring Him,
      Nearer His heart.

The foxes have their holes, the wise, the clever;
The birds have each a safe and secret nest;
But He, my lover, walks the world with never
      A place to rest.

I found Him once upon a straw bed lying;
Once on His mother's heart He laid His head;
He had a bramble pillow for His dying,
      A stone when dead.

I think to leave off singing for this reason,
Taking instead my Lord God's house to keep,
Where He may find a home in every season
      To wake, to sleep.

Do you not think that in this holy sweetness
Of silence shared with God a whole life long
Both He and I shall find divine completeness
Of perfect song?

CANDLE-LIGHT

Day has its sun,
And night the stars,
But God has candle-light.

Upon the world's great candle-stick He sets
The little taper of yourself ashine,
That when the sun has sputtered out
And all the stars are dead,
Your immortality may flame and burn
Across His infinite immensity forever.

Wherefore He will sometime blow out the sun,
And snuff the stars,
Preferring candle-light.

SUMMARIES

PRESENTATION

Two doves I bring;
One broods all day;
One has a broken wing;
One is the prayer I have no words to say;
One is the song I have no words to sing.

HONEY

Mary is the flower-field where
Bernard, the bee,
Drinks wild nectar to
Ecstasy.

FIRE

Dominic, the dog, his
Mouth aflame,
Is a firebrand lighted at
Mary's name.

DUMB OXEN

Mary, pray for Paris
And Bethlehem;
A dumb ox served you
In both of them.

PASSOVER NIGHT: MARY SPEAKS

Once I bought my Son back with
Pigeons white.
O Judas, have we no
Doves tonight?

FOOD FOR SAILORS

Odysseus ate the lotus with his crew,
Forgot their home and thought that they were swine.
Who taste the flower of Jesse's blossoming rod
Remember Eden, know they are divine.

SPEAKING OF HONEST MEN

Blow out your foolish lamp; here are two honest men,
Diogenes;
A thief and a blasphemer, or, I think, a god,
On gallows-trees.

DREAMS OF THE ROOD

FERRY MAN

Christopher is Christ's ferry man
Across the flood.
I stand with arms outstretched and wide
And am Christ's rood.

HUNTER'S LICENSE

Midway above your antlered head,
Beautiful buck, Christ's cross is set.
There Eustace saw it shining once
And I can see it yet.

PARAPHRASE FROM THE "NUN'S RULE"

By quaint ways men keep things in thought.
Our sweet Lord Christ, to mind Him of us,
Wears piercing marks in hands and feet,
The more to love us.

THE CHERRY TREE

The world is filled with You!
From what besides Your beauty could I have fashioned
    flower-buds?
Tomorrow You shall have cherry-blossoms, my Maker.

OPINION

If all the sky should quiver into pinions,
And all the air should tinkle into silver singing,
The earth would still have need, I think, for bluebirds.

CONCERNING DEATH

ENLIGHTENMENT

My moonlit night is a young girl, death-sick, pale,
With candles dimly burning at her bed. The dawn will
    come to fetch her.
Meanwhile I wait and watch, thinking to learn another
    lovely thing of death.

I ASK MY TEACHERS

Why do you wrap your wisdom in a multitude of words?
My master, death, who will enlighten me completely
    and forever,
Employs no speech at all.

THE DAY NO LETTER COMES

The day you do not write and silence follows, to be
    broken only by my life's end,
I shall know that you have not forgotten, that now you
    love me perfectly,
For I shall understand that you are dead.

71

DEATH

The moon does not change.
Tonight a shadow shuts from me its borrowed beauty!
This will be divinely true of you when you are dead.

STATEMENT

Nothing caught fire from the moon
Smouldering on the east horizon.
Three gaunt boughs of the sycamore
Were charred by night against it
And the banked embers of its splendor
Burn in my memory yet.

A CHILD ASLEEP

This is the child you trusted to my keeping,
Remote, mysterious as all shy things are.
Against her heart the summer night is sleeping,
Against her lips the stillness of a star.

SONG

You are the young moon's bright
Joy in the innocent white
Snow, are the stars' delight
In their deep heaven's height.
Sweet, read my song aright.
You are my love. Good night.

CALENDAR

MARCH

Of what tumultuous grief these tears are token!
I wipe them with the wind which is my hair;
And now my alabaster box is broken,
Spilling the breath of lilies everywhere.

Winter, my Lord, let all the seasons tell
I do these things against your burial.

AT WINTER'S END

Buds are backward and winter lingers
But you, the eager, the quick, the wary,
Have found the first gold fritillary,
The clustered, rose-pink lady-fingers.

You have found, too, with cautious hunting,
That tricky one, the elusive towhee,
The tanager, splendidly shy and showy,
The summer-minded lazuli bunting.

I come not back with April weather;
Winds cannot woo nor sun unbind me.
Much as you seek, you cannot find me;
We shall not have this spring together.

But we warm our hearts at no dying ember.
Who can tell us how love is parted?
We are forever happy-hearted,
Having one springtime to remember.

CONCEIT

If lovers could make summer, could make spring,
What delicate gifts at dawn, at evening
To tremulous sweethearts would all suitors bring!

And think how fine, how loverlike to say,
"Prithee, wilt take my posy, sweet; 'tis May?"
Or, "With my heart I bring thee June today."

Dearer than any light on land or sea
This thing has come to pass. Exquisitely
My love is making April just for me.

AUTUMN

For that I dreamed the night long of my lover
I must be clad today most radiantly.
Come, earth and air and sky;
Put all my outworn summer raiment by.
Gold I will wear
For all my golden dreams of him and fair;
And red,
The burning memory of one beauteous word he said.
Sky, earth, and air,
Think you my love is come, the importunate rover?
Quick, fetch me a mist of purple for my hair,
And for my hand
A single snowflake flower,
Sign of my passing hour.
See how all beautiful I stand
Waiting—ah! who could guess—waiting for death, my
    lover.

PIED PIPER

Brave Piper October, what tune do you blow
That the leaves are bewitched and wherever you go
They flutter and follow, agleam and aglow?
From oak tree and bramble, from high tree and low
They flock to the sound of the piping they know,
And down from the tall trees of heaven, O ho!
Come dancing and glancing the white leaves of snow.

SWADDLING CLOTHES

My days are all white with wonder, the wonder of stitch-
    ing and sewing,
Making a spotless garment for Mary's spotless Son;
My hours are bright with joy as I watch the small robe
    growing,
The little robe of love that will compass the infinite One.
Love is the cloth it is made from; my heart possesseth no
    other;
Love is the pattern, too, that I trace with unfaltering
    care;
Love is my double thread, the love of the Son and the
    mother;
Woven throughout of love, think you it will be fair?
Aye, and the mother Mary will let her little One wear it,
He Who hath never in aught save divinity been arrayed,
All upon Christmas morning; O heart of me, canst thou
    bear it,
The joy of thy God appareled in raiment thy love hath
    made!

POSSESSION

I cannot chant the angels' hymn
As did the hosts of seraphim.

I cannot even cross the wild
As shepherds did, to find the Child.

I cannot shine, a living star,
To guide grave magi from afar.

I have no incense, myrrh, or gold
For gift as had the kings of old.

In all the world there is nowhere
A place so poor, a spot so bare,

Save the rude cave at Bethlehem town
Where Christ, my Savior, laid Him down.

For that I am like that mean stall
I may possess Him most of all.

CHRISTMAS: ELIZABETH WATCHES THE NIGHT SKY

I think the clouds tonight
Are lambs and wayward sheep,
Huddled and lost and white.
My boy stirs in his sleep!

At midnight he awoke
As at an uttered word.
I only guess who spoke
And what he heard.

His eyes, before he slept,
Grew deep as prophets' are.
Up from their darkness leapt
Light like a star.

Two clouds drift in the blue.
How strangely moved I am!
They are like a lone ewe
And her young lamb.

CHRISTMAS EVE

I journeyed down to Bethlehem
In deep peace on a winter day.
I think a young girl and a man
Were with me on the way.

And in the little town at dusk
The young girl waited in the street.
The stones and I were very glad
With kissing of her feet.

A tender wind encompassed her;
The waiting world, the listening air,
The watching stars grew sweet and white
With kissing of her hair.

The earth was wise as any child
Because she was so young and wise
And all the dark was luminous
With looking in her eyes.

Tonight I wait upon my knees
Beside her in this quiet place,
Loving the wonder in her heart,
The wonder in her face.

WISHES

The Christmas stars at Bethlehem
Shone very clear and bright;
Oh, may they shine with light divine
For you this Christmas night!

The Christmas winds at Bethlehem
Folded their wings away;
May every wind blow gently kind
For you on Christmas day.

The angel hosts at Bethlehem
Sang "Peace on earth to men";
And may their song ring loud and long
Within your heart again.

The shepherds come to Bethlehem
Knelt in rapt wondering;
To Bethlehem, oh, haste with them
To see the little King!

The holy pair at Bethlehem
Looked upon them and smiled;
Would it might be your lot to see
These blest ones and the Child.

88

The little Babe at Bethlehem
Gave them His hand to kiss;
And oh, I pray your heart today
May know such joy as this.

A NUN SPEAKS TO MARY

I

In the Days of King Herod

You had no little maid, so I remember,
To help you sweep and tidy up the room,
To sit and watch with you that first December
Through shining twilights deep with golden gloom.

Through all those wistful days you had no mother
To know your wonder and to share your joy
Of fashioning—you could not let another!—
The darling swaddling garments for your Boy.

There was not any housewife to befriend you
The day word came to go to Bethlehem town;
No kinswoman bethought her to attend you
Of all the folk of David going down.

And when you held Him to your heart in wonder,
Emmanuel, God's Son, your Boy, the Word
Made flesh Who shook the skies with holy thunder,
In Bethlehem not any mother stirred.

II

SEQUEL

Now come again the sweet Isaian days,
Merciful, tender;
I know their loneliness; I dream their splendor.
Down their plain ways,
Mary, I come,
Confounded with this former shame, and dumb.
Take me in service, in complete surrender,
Waking and sleeping;
Take every daily task; take every duty;
Take little homely things as dusting, sweeping;
Change them into your heavenly housekeeping;
Touch them with Nazareth's most stricken beauty.
Think that my busy hands weave raiment fair
For Christ to wear;
Know that my hurrying feet
Run all your errands, Sweet;
And should they tarry,
Hear how I promise them,
My Lady Mary,
That they at length may go with you to Bethlehem.

And at the last let be
On those three mute and piteous, fearful days
When none of all earth's womenfolk is near you,
That you will have to help you and to cheer you
In little foolish ways
Poor, simple me;
That when you stand outside the inn, the night wind
  blowing,
I will be there
Adoring, knowing;
That if the whole wide world should have no room,
I will be waiting through whatever gloom
To be your resting place. But this is heaven I dare!

So, let my promise be my prayer.
And do not seek for any cave at all
With patient kine and manger crib and stall
Beyond the gates of little Bethlehem town
To lay your dear Son down.
Mother, all fair,
Lay Him within my hungry arms to sleep;
Lay Him within my hungry heart to keep,
Adorable, holy,
Little and lowly.

And let earth's shepherds, let heaven's seraphim
So find me with you Christmas night, adoring, loving
   Him.

BALLAD OF THE HAPPY CHRISTMAS WIND

I am a happy Christmas wind;
I am courteous; I am kind.

I walked the way to Bethlehem town
Beside our Lady going down.

I know the inn she stood before;
I would have beaten down the door;

I thought on Mary and the Child;
I blew gently; I grew mild.

I ran ahead to find a house
To shelter Mary and her spouse.

I found a stable, loosed the door,
The cave they had been seeking for.

Because they had a place to bide
I was so glad, alone outside,

I ran across the hills for joy!
I waked a little shepherd boy,

And all the older shepherds stirred
At what they felt and what they heard

Of angel music, heavenly things!
I caught the song and gave it wings;

I ran across the midnight blue;
I ran across the ages, too;
I have it, have it here for you.

A Child is born for you again;
A Son is given, is given to men!
I am a singing wind. Amen.

SONNETS

HYÈRES
(From Sainte Claire Le Chateau *)

This is no city lying at my feet.
It is, I think, some bravely blazoned shield,
Fair as the sun and by the sun annealed;
Its proud device of avenue and street
A hundred palms and plantane trees repeat;
Vermilion roofs upon an azure field
Quartered with garden greens, and, wonder-keeled,
The ocean, argent, crescent, incomplete.

There are so many things that one forgets,
But never this sun-smitten shield of France
With, for its crest, rampant against the sky,
A single eucalyptus, greaved and high,
And, couchant at the heart of old romance,
Field upon field of breathing violets.

* The home of Edith Wharton.

CHRISTMAS IN PROVENÇE

Midnight Mass

Tonight this city seated on a hill
Wears its medieval fortress like a crown
Above a brow too peace-possessed to frown.
Its ancient church watches the darkness fill
With quiet aureoles of light that spill
Through little streets that clamber up the town.
Here ancient, royal kings have laid them down,
And here, this night, a King will rest Him still.

I had not known that night could be so holy;
I had not thought that peace could be so deep.
O passion of night and peace, possess me solely!
O passion of love, be mine this night to keep!
O little climbing streets, lead me up slowly
To where the King I wait for lies asleep!

CHRISTMAS IN PROVENÇE

THE SERENADE

This age-old church, dream-stricken yesterday,
Has wakened into loveliness and light
And all Provençe is in its arms tonight
And all its tambourines and fifes are gay.
The dull, encumbering ages fall away;
Templar and king kneel in the ancient rite
With torches' blaze and candles tall and white
And a Child cradled on the fresh-strewn hay.

Then the night fills with song, laughing and leaping,
This music of a thousand lyric years;
A serenade of love where love lies sleeping,
The minstrelsy of God where God appears,
And where I kneel, bemused, song-shaken, weeping,
A happy-hearted troubadour in tears.

MID-OCEAN

We know our mountains well, their winds, their weather.
Horizons high and white in the heavenly hush
Of sun- or moonlit snow; the ecstatic rush
Of pentecostal spring in leaf and feather;
Wild altitudes of blossoming summer, whether
Cliff rose, pentstemon's blue, or lupine's flush;
Autumn's apocalyptic burning bush :
All these we have loved rapturously together.

Sometime, beloved, we shall see the ocean,
Not continents apart and separately;
Then all this passionate peace, this passionate motion,
Wonder, omnipotence, immensity,
We shall possess beyond all word, all notion,
Silent, together, looking out to sea.

OLD SOLDIERS

Look at this avenue. Do you not love it,
This regiment of trees in ranks of fours
Marching abreast, maples and sycamores?
It is a body-guard a king could covet.
I like its strength, but most, the beauty of it,
And this one thing too mere for metaphors,
Its gray-black-white with winter out-of-doors,
And any winter sky at all above it.

There is one austere veteran; you must know **him,**
That grave, gaunt sycamore, battered and white
And standing stark beneath the blue of noon.
What a fine debt of dignity we owe him!
But wait until you watch him through the **night;**
Wait till you see him sharp against the **moon.**

BEECH TREES

I passed a wood of beech trees yesterday
And I am shaken with its beauty yet.
Why should my breath catch and my eyes be wet
Because a hundred trees some yards away
Know simply how to dress in simple gray,
Are poised beyond the need of epithet,
And beautiful past power to forget?
I dare not think how they will look in May.

They wore illustrious yellow in the fall.
Their beauty is no thing at which they guess.
And when they put on green, and when they carry
Fans open in the sun or folded small,
I'll look through tears at ultimate loveliness:
Beeches in May, beeches in February.

STONEHENGE

This may have been a temple to the sun,
This enigmatic pile of Druid stone.
Across its western portal may have shone
The springtime dawn that lighted Babylon.
Something like this the pharaohs might have done,
Imposing rock on rock, erect or prone,
Inert, bloodstained, wind-beaten, weather-blown,
In dogged protest to oblivion.

Not with such stolid ponderosity
Do I adore the light and love the sky.
Fluttering from tangled grasses at my feet
A skylark, fugitive and silver-sweet,
My worship is, or southward, lifted high,
The simple lyric spire of Salisbury.

EASTER CHRONICLE

Today is Easter; I am at Solesmes.
The air is still and delicate and sweet.
Violets cloud the path before my feet
And edge the village with their purple hem.
Alone, bemused with song, I gather them,
Thinking how, on this morning, I should meet
Blossoming sound, antiphonal, complete,
Blossoming color, leaf and flower and stem.

It has unfolded for me like a flower,
This great Gregorian chant: the solemn Mass,
The morning Office, hour by heavenly hour.
There shall remain when lesser praise shall pass
This music that is peace and prayer and power,
These April violets in the quickened grass.

CALIFORNIA SPRING

Such spring as one has need of here is ended,
With signs scarce marked and mercifully few:
Leaves for the eucalyptus, white and new;
The threadbare hills with great, green patches mended,
But not as if a new world were intended.
What need? And so I watch the noon's high blue
And dare, with April here, to think of you.
Suppose the acacia were more subtly splendid!

Suppose such life, such beauty, hour by hour
Came creeping on me, stealthily, like a thief!
What weapon have I for a gradual flower
Or what defense against a folded leaf;
To parry long, sure thoughts of you what power?
Yes, spring has shown me mercy, being brief.

RETURN

This is your home to which you are returning.
Because you have so hungered for the place,
Shall we not stop to say the simple grace
That you have spent a passionate lifetime learning?
Upon the hearth a brave, new fire is burning;
The flowers you hoped would greet you in the vase
You wished, are here; here that grave, tender face
You tell me is the sum of all your yearning.

The threshold's peace, impatient to possess you,
More lovely than, homesick, you clamored for;
Music at once to shatter and caress you;
The voice you dream; the hands that you adore;
All, all are here to welcome and to bless you.
Come to my waiting heart! What will you more?

MARGINALIUM

I think the story of Shalott is wrong.
Oh! not the "four gray walls and four gray towers,"
The placid isle and prettiness of flowers,
Nor the sweet incongruity of song.
The river slipping by the summer long,
The lads and lasses, barley fields and bowers,
The listless maid, weaving the livelong hours,
The knight: all these are proper; these belong.

But not youth cursed by love, unwitting how,
Drifting to death upon a senseless tide!
Girl, let your mirror break, your web blow wide;
Nail love's bright flag with life's upon your prow.
Know that you have not ever lived till now.
Who said that love would curse and kill you, lied.

IF YOU WOULD HOLD ME

It is so very strange that, loving me,
You should ensnare the freedom I find sweet,
Catch in your cunning will my flying feet.
I will not barter love for liberty;
You cannot break and tame me utterly;
For when your careful conquest is complete
Shall victory be swallowed in defeat.
You hold me only when you set me free.

Because my straight, wild ways are in your power
Do not believe that I surrender them.
Untrammeled love is all I have to give.
If you would keep it, do not pluck the flower;
Leave it, I beg, unbroken on its stem,
Wild with the wind and weather. Let it live!

ON THIS CONDITION

Oh, do I love you? Yes, to be brief and plain.
But from my window, if the day is clear,
See that far mountain, lonely and austere,
Flush into gradual wonder, where has lain
Passionless, pallid snow. Almost like pain
Rose-splendid radiance wraps it in beauty sheer
As the sun kisses it—wait, wait, my dear—
And passing, leaves it virgin white again.

When we have reached those heights of calm surrender
Where white integrity and love are one,
Then you may compass me with utter splendor,
Nor shall we need to wish our joy undone.
Then you may kiss me, love, or tense or tender;
Then you may shine on me, being my sun.

PATRINS

Yes, I shall leave these patrins as I go:
Plucked grasses here, a few blown blossoms there,
To tell you, though I've gone, how much I care;
To tell you, also, should you want to know,
The way I've taken, my beloved, so
That you can find me, find me anywhere.
Be still, my heart! You know he does not dare
To follow dreams; have you no signs to show?

Only the wide, white comfort of the stars,
And strange, lone rest within the arms of dawn,
And love that binds, and truth that sets me free.
Why should you fear such infinite prison bars?
The wild and wistful way that I have gone
Leads but to peace. Beloved, follow me.

OCTOBER BIRTHDAY

Were I immortal only I would proffer
Tokens tremendous as a god can give:
Planets in leash, an earth whereon to live
With all October's fugitive gold in coffer,
Its moon a sorceress, its wind a scoffer,
Oceans it carries in a sandy sieve,
And stars aloof and undemonstrative.
Gifts casually infinite I could offer.

But as a woman and your love I bring you
The simple, homely things a woman must:
A little, human-hearted song to sing you,
My arms to comfort and my lips to trust;
The tangled moods that, autumn-wise, I fling you;
The frail and faulty tenderness of dust.

TRIBUTE

I have known mountains when the day was new
Clothed beyond beauty's self in morning splendor;
Have seen them stand like queens, serene and tender,
Against noon's high tranquillity of blue.
I have watched purple mists and rose-white dew
Cling to them and the young moon, frail and slender,
Shed on them silver homage of surrender.
I have known this of mountains and of you.

You are the majesty of all my days,
Set in an aureole of morning light,
Set in my life's high noon; against its night
You will be yet the beauty of my ways.
Ah, let me be the moon, crescent and white,
Shining before you, mute with love and praise!

ULTIMATES

Although you know, you cannot end my quest,
Nor ever, ever compass my desire;
That were to burn me with divinest fire;
That were to fill me with divinest rest,
To lift me, living, to God's living breast.
I should not dare this thing, nor you aspire
To it, who no less passionately require
Love ultimate, possessor and possessed.

You who are everything and are not this,
Be but its dream, its utter, sweet surmise
Which waking makes the more intensely true
With every exquisite, wistful part of you;
My own, the depths of your untroubled eyes,
Your quiet hands, and your most quiet kiss.

THE YOUNG PRIEST'S MOTHER

Yes, he is mine if miracles of weaving
Flesh from my flesh and blood into the fine
Potencies of white manhood, every line
Perfect past mute desire or proud believing
Can make him; if the mystery of achieving
Out of a human son this son divine
Owes aught to motherhood, then he is mine
Beyond my body's gift, my soul's conceiving.

And I am his beyond the extremest guesses
Of men, bound by indissoluble bands
Forever. It is not only he who blesses
And holds me close, but O he understands
Why adoration burns in my caresses,
What wounds I kiss upon his beautiful hands!

MIRRORS

I seek you always. Have I never seen you?
Let's ask if any bird has seen the air,
Or flower the light, though these are everywhere.
Choose any veil you will. Set it between you
And my beholding. Know it shall not screen you
From me. What occult vestures you may wear,
Too dread or dull or difficult to bear,
Are mirrors meaning naught unless they mean you?

Is beauty something I cannot discover?
Is truth a thing that only children know?
Are you not mine who are the whole world's lover?
Can I not find you in all winds that blow,
In the wild loneliness of lark and plover,
In slender shadow trees upon the snow?

MY BEST DRESS

This dress I wear with absolute, heavenly grace.
A hundred gowns I've wished for, asked or hinted;
A hundred fabrics dreamed of, plain or printed.
But witcheries of linen, lawn, and lace
Are mere accessories to these hands, this face,
This body whole, with naught amiss or stinted;
Made of a stuff of clay, divinely minted,
And textured through with life and time and place.

My mother wove it from her loveliness.
She wished it perfect; she assumed it brave.
Today, which is my life, I wear the dress
With the fierce pride and dignity she gave.
At night will some one take it, please, and bless
And put it neatly for her in my grave?

DETAILS FOR MY BURIAL

As for the matter of my burial
It follows hard the golden day I die.
There needs but a small grave where I may lie,
Cut in the snow's white peace I love so well,
Or sweetened with young rain—one cannot tell—
But always, always the great, solicitous sky,
The quick, close earth, and all that live thereby.
Dear God, how I desire the consecrate cell!

It holds divine reprieves, immortal pardons
Whereby my vagabond feet are stricken free;
My fingers busy here with mortal gardens
May plant and pluck to ultimate ecstasy.
Myself? A heavenly tramp in heavenly Ardens!
Remember, when you dig a grave for me.